Honey

By Julie Haydon

Contents

Honey Bees

Honey bees are insects.
They have three body parts and six legs.
Honey bees have four wings, too.

Honey bees on farms live in nests called hives.

Most of the bees in a hive are worker bees.
Worker bees are female.
Worker bees do most of the work
in and out of the hive.

a hive

Worker bees leave the hive
to collect nectar and pollen
from flowers.

Nectar is the sweet juice
inside flowers.

Pollen is a yellow powder
on flowers.

When the worker bees return to the hive, other worker bees turn the nectar into honey.

The honey and pollen are stored in the hive.

Worker bees make honey comb inside the hive.

Honey comb is made of wax and is full of little holes.

Worker bees store the honey and pollen in the holes.

Bees eat honey and pollen all year.
They store the honey and pollen
when there are lots of flowers.

In colder months,
bees eat the honey and pollen
they have stored.

One queen bee lives in each hive.
The queen bee is bigger than the other bees
in the hive.
She lays eggs in the holes in the comb.
Baby bees come out of the eggs.

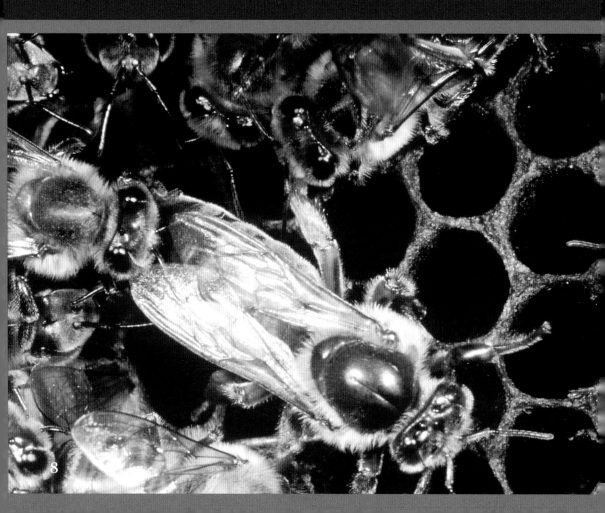

The male bees in a hive are called drones.
Drones have eyes that are much larger
than the eyes of worker bees.
The drones mate with the queen.

Honey bees are very interesting insects
to study.

A Letter to Sophie

Dear Sophie,

This year we had a good summer on the farm.
Our honey bees made lots of honey.

Our bees were in their hives for most of the winter. It was too cold for them to fly around outside.

In spring, we saw the worker bees
flying from flower to flower.
They got nectar from the flowers.
They took the nectar back to the hives
where other worker bees turned it into honey.

Sometimes, we saw the worker bees getting pollen from flowers.
The bees put the pollen in little bags on their back legs.
The bees took the pollen back to the hives.

The bees in the hives
ate some of the honey and pollen.
The rest of it was stored in the honey comb
to be eaten later.

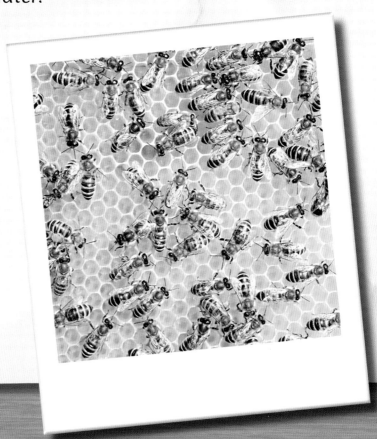

I opened the hives in summer
and collected some of the honey.

This year, the bees were very busy.
They made lots of honey.

I have sent you a pot of honey.

I hope you enjoy it.

Love from,
Uncle Dan